Notable Knit
LACE

Complete Instructions
for **6 Projects**

Creative Publishing
international

contents

ABBREVIATIONS

Here is the list of standard abbreviations used for knitting. Until you can readily identify them, keep the list handy whenever you knit.

beg . . . . begin

bet . . . . between

BO . . . . bind off

CC . . . . contrasting color

cm . . . . centimeter

cn . . . . cable needle

CO . . . . cast on

Col . . . . color

cont . . . . continue

dec . . . . decrease

dpn . . . . double-pointed needle(s)

g . . . . grams

inc . . . . increase

k . . . . knit

k1f&b . . . . knit into front and back loop of same stitch

k2tog . . . . knit two stitches together

kwise . . . . knitwise

m(s) . . . . markers(s)

MC . . . . main color

rem . . . . remaining or remain

rep . . . . repeat

mm . . . . millimeters

M1 . . . . make one stitch (increase)

oz . . . . ounce

p . . . . purl

p1f&b . . . . purl into front and back loop of same stitch

p2tog . . . . purl two stitches together

patt . . . . pattern

pm . . . . place marker

psso . . . . pass slipped stitch over

pwise . . . . purlwise

rep . . . . repeat

rev St st . . . . . reverse stockinette stitch

rib . . . . ribbing

rnd(s) . . . . rounds

RS . . . . right side

sk . . . . skip

skp . . . . slip 1, knit 1, pass slipped stitch over (decrease)

sl . . . . slip

sl1k . . . . slip one knitwise

sl1p . . . . slip one purlwise

sl st . . . . slip stitch

sm . . . . slip marker

ssk . . . . slip 1, slip 1, knit these 2 stitches together (decrease)

st(s) . . . . stitch(es)

St st . . . . stockinette stitch

tbl . . . . through back loop

tog . . . . together

WS . . . . wrong side

wyb . . . . with yarn in back

wyf . . . . with yarn in front

yb . . . . yarn back

yf . . . . yarn forward

yo . . . . yarn over needle

* . . . . repeat from *

[ ] . . . . repeat instructions in brackets as directed

( ) . . . . repeat instructions in parentheses as directed

( ) . . . . number of stitches that should be on the needle or across a row

Lace Scarf with Beaded Edge

A very easy lace pattern is used to create this stunning scarf made from hand-dyed sock weight yarn. The bottom edges are accented with a subtle row of beads that are added while casting on. Two identical halves are made and joined in the middle of the scarf so that both ends are accented with scallops. Scarf instructions begin on page 158.

WHAT YOU'LL LEARN . . . .

- How to make a beaded cast-on edge
- How to make a simple lace pattern
- How to make a double decrease (psso)
- How to join two scarf halves with three-needle bind-off
- How to block lace

WHAT YOU'LL NEED . . . .

YARN

- Super fine weight, smooth yarn, approx. 300 yd (274 m).

  Either wind the yarn into two balls of equal weight or weigh the total yarn before beginning knitting so you will know when approximately half the yarn is used and the second half of the scarf should be started.

NEEDLES AND NOTIONS

- US size 5 (3.75 mm) needles or size needed to achieve gauge, 2 sets
- US size 6 (4 mm) needle or one size larger that size needed to achieve gauge for three-needle bind-off
- Beading needle, big eye style, at least 2" (5 cm) long
- Seed beads, size 6 (3.3 mm); at least 62 beads in colors to coordinate with yarn
-

- Circular stitch markers
- Yarn needle for weaving in ends
- Rustproof T-pins for blocking
- Tape measure

EQUIPMENT

- Iron
- Ironing board
- Blocking board or carpeted floor
- Towel

GAUGE

- 20 sts = 4" (10 cm) in stockinette stitch
- 23 sts = 4" (10 cm) in lace pattern

Skills and Useful Information

PASS SLIPPED STITCH OVER (PSSO)

This is a technique that is used in combination with a k2tog decrease to create a double (2-stitch) decrease.

1 Slip 1 stitch from the left needle to the right needle. To do so, insert the right needle into the first stitch on the left needle as if getting ready to knit and slip it off the left needle an on to the right needle.

2 Knit the next 2 stitches together (k2tog) as if they were one.

3 Use the left needle to pass the slipped stitch over the decreased stitch and off the end of the needle. Two stitches have been decreased. Note: if a simple knit stitch (instead of k2tog) is combined with a psso, then only one stitch is decreased.

BLOCKING LACE

Lace must be blocked in some manner once finished or else it will have a bumpy surface texture and uneven edges. Start by blocking lace using steam, as described below. In most cases the lace will require additional blocking. Pin the lace to a blocking board, carpeted surface, or bed mattress and cover it with a damp towel or enclose it in a sandwich of two damp towels.

BLOCKING LACE

If the lace item you are blocking is small enough, you can start the process with steam blocking. A steam iron or steamer is used to penetrate your knit piece with steam that relaxes the fibers and evens out the stitches. At no point should the steam iron actually touch the knitting—it should be held an inch (2.5 cm) above.

1 Spread the item to be blocked on your ironing board or another heat-resistant flat surface and, working in sections, hold the iron above the item, allowing the steam to penetrate the work. Set the iron aside and use your hands to gently stretch and smooth the lace until it lies flat. Also, smooth and stretch any straight edges and coax the scallops into gentle points. Note: if you have any doubts about using steam, then skip this step.

2 Once the item has been steamed, lay it on a blocking board, carpeted floor, or bed mattress and smooth the item into shape. Use rustproof T-pins to pin the item to the blocking surface, beginning with the corners. Use a tape measure to make sure the width and length are consistent. Continue by pinning all the edges at frequent intervals. Also, place a pin in each scallop point (A). Cover the entire item with a towel that is just barely wet (wet the towel in the washer and then spin it dry) (B). Leave the towel in place until the item is completely dry.

3 If desired, blocking wires (long, semiflexible lengths of wire) can be used along straight edges to avoid creating tiny puckers from the pins. The wires are threaded along the straight edges. Instead of pinning the knitting, the wires are held in place using a few pins. This method is quite fast and gives a smoother straight edge.

2A

2B

3

STITCH MARKERS

Stitch markers play a very important role in lace knitting. Typically, lace is composed of an identical set of stitches that are repeated over and over across the width of the item. Markers are used to delineate each set of identical stitches. For instance, the Lace Curtain Panels (page 28) are made using a 10-stitch lace pattern that is repeated a total of seven times from side to side. Each 10-stitch section is enclosed by markers. When you reach a marker while knitting a row, slip it from the left needle to the right needle (sm—slip marker) and continue with the next repeat. Until you become proficient with the pattern, at the end of each row, count the stitches to make sure you have the same number between each set of markers. You will quickly memorize which stitch should be coming up in relation to the stitch marker. This will help you to find and correct mistakes within a particular repeat rather than discovering at the end of a row that you have too many or too few stitches.

THREE-NEEDLE BIND-OFF

The three-needle bind-off is used to make a seam and bind off two edges simultaneously. It can be used, for instance, to join two halves of a scarf or join a shoulder seam. **The two pieces being joined must have the same number of stitches.** The third needle that is used for the bind-off step should be one size larger than that used for the knitting. (Note that in the photographs the yarn used for working the stitches is a different color in order to show contrast. You should use the same color yarn as the pieces being joined).

To prepare for the three-needle bind-off, knit the two pieces to be joined through the last row before the bind-off. Because the needle tips must be pointed in the same direction, it will necessitate ending one side on a wrong-side row and the other side on a right-side row. Alternatively, if you are using a circular needle, the stitches of one side can be pushed across the needle so that the needle points and the knit edges line up. This will allow you to end each side on the same row. Don't bind off the stitches but leave them on the needle. The yarn from one of the sides can be cut, leaving a tail at least 8" (20 cm) long. Do not cut the yarn from the other side.

1 Place the two pieces of knitting so that the **right sides are together** and the two needles are held parallel to each other with the tips pointing to the right.

2 Insert the third needle into the first stitch on both the front and back needle as if to make a knit stitch.

3 Using the working yarn that remains from the last row of knitting, wrap the yarn around the third needle and draw the loop through both of the stitches on the front and back needles, thus knitting the 2 stitches together and allowing them to slip off the needles.

4 Knit the next 2 stitches (one on the front needle and one on the back needle) in the same manner. There will now be 2 stitches on the third, or right-hand, needle.

5 Using one of the needles in your left hand, pass the right stitch on the third needle over the left stitch (the one closest to the needle tip) and off the end of the needle. One stitch has been bound off.

Repeat steps 2 to 5 until just one loop remains on the third needle. Cut the yarn leaving a tail at least 8" (20 cm) long and pull the cut end through the last stitch to secure it.

How to Knit the Lace Scarf with Beaded Edge

It's easy to modify the width of the scarf. Each repeat of the lace pattern is 7 stitches and about 2" (5 cm) wide. Change the width of the scarf by adding or subtracting stitches in multiples of 7.

KNIT THE SCARF SECTIONS (MAKE TWO ALIKE, EACH USING HALF OF THE TOTAL YARN)
Thread Beads onto the Yarn Using the Big Eye Needle.

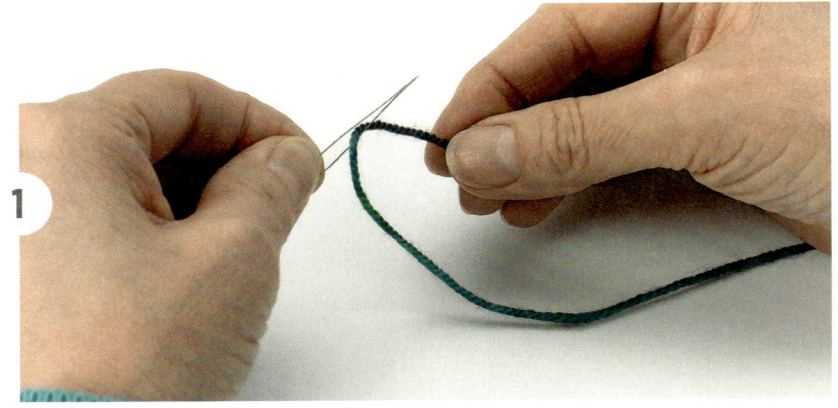

1 Before making the cast-on row, 32 beads must be threaded onto the yarn. The big eye beading needle has a large slit (the eye) in the middle. Pry the slit open with your fingernail or another needle and thread the yarn through the needle slit, leaving a short tail.

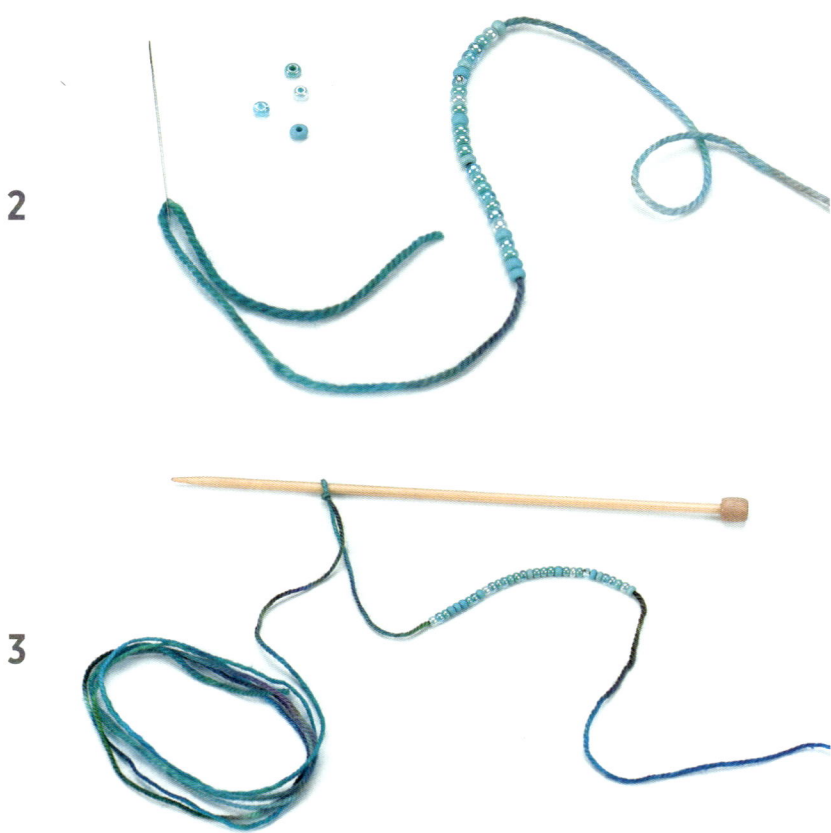

2 Insert the pointed end of the big eye needle through the bead and then slide the bead onto the yarn. Once 32 beads have been strung, remove the beading needle and slide all of the beads at least 1 yd (91 cm) away from the end of the yarn.

3 Make a slip knot in the yarn to the left of the threaded beads and place the slip knot on the knitting needle. The tail for the cast-on (1 yd [91 cm] long) will be to the left of the slip knot, and the threaded beads and working yarn will be to the right of the slip knot. The beads should be about 8" (20 cm) away from the slip knot.

TIP Slip the stitch markers as you come to them. Until you become comfortable with the pattern, it helps to count the 7 stitches in each section after completion.

Make Beaded Cast-on

Every other cast-on stitch will include a bead. Think of it as working the cast-on stitches in pairs using a two-step process.

Step 1: Cast on 1 st.

Step 2: Slide a bead up against the needle and keep it snug against the needle with the index finger of your right hand (A) while casting on the next stitch with your left hand (B).

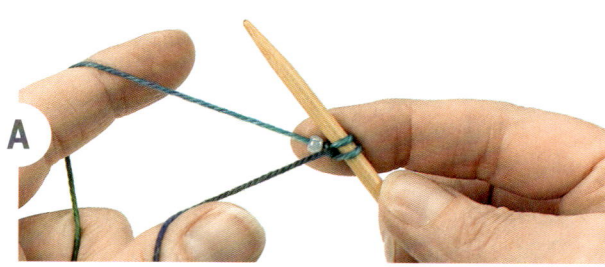

Repeat steps 1 and 2 over and over until all 32 beads have been worked into the cast-on row. End with one more (plain) cast on stitch. You will have 65 stitches (loops) on the needle.

Decrease Stitches and Work Set-up Row

The number of stitches for the scarf must be decreased by half and finally a set-up row is worked to place markers (pm) to delineate the lace pattern repeats.

Row 1: Purl.

Row 2: K1, *k2tog*; repeat from * to * to end of row; 33 sts remain.

Row 3: P1, p2tog, *pm, p7*; repeat from * to * until 2 sts remain, pm, p2; 32 sts remain.

Begin Lace Pattern

The lace pattern itself is an easy 2-row repeat. Each pattern repeat is 7 stitches wide from side to side, and there are 2 stitches at each edge of the scarf.

Row 1 (RS): K1, p1, *sm, k1, yo, ssk, k1, k2tog, yo, k1* repeat from * to * until 2 sts remain, sm, p1, k1.

Row 2: Purl.

Repeat rows 1 and 2 until half of the yarn is used up (see yarn note on page 5 in the What You'll Need). After completing the last row 2, set the first scarf half aside, leaving the stitches on the needle.

Using the additional set of needles make a second scarf half identical to the first following the steps outlined above for threading the beads onto the yarn, the beaded cast-on, the set-up row, and the lace pattern. For the second scarf section only, one additional row must be completed as follows:

Next row: Knit.

Leave the stitches of the second scarf half on the needle after completing the additional row.

Join Scarf Halves Together

Hold the scarf halves so that the right sides are together and the two needles are held parallel to each other with the tips pointing to the right. The wrong sides of the knitting distinguished by the bumpy, purl texture will be facing the outside. Using a third needle that is one size larger, work a three-needle bind-off to join the two halves together.

Block following the directions on page 155 for blocking lace.

Your Feminine Side

RUFFLES AND LACE

Ruffles, lace, and drama. When you wear this shawl to your next party, be sure to arrive late—you wouldn't want to waste a wrap this gorgeous with a punctual arrival. This shawl will allow you to use several skills on the same project. You'll be knitting sideways on a circular needle, beginning and ending with a ruffle, and the body is an easy lace stitch. It's not as tricky as it sounds, but there is one step that might make you nervous. You need to cast on a lot of stitches for the bottom ruffle—a whole lot of stitches. That's why you need such a long needle; it's the only way to fit all of the beginning stitches. In Knitting Class on page 16, you will learn two tricks to make casting on the stitches easier.

YARN

Lightweight smooth rayon yarn: 875 yd (800 m)

NEEDLES AND NOTIONS

- Size 6 (4 mm) circular needle or size needed to obtain gauge, at least 40" (102 cm) long
- Blunt-end yarn needle

GAUGE

- 19 stitches = 4" (10 cm) in lace stitch

FINISHED SIZE

- 11" × 72" (28 × 183 cm)

TIP When you are knitting with lots of stitches, it's easy to accidentally add a stitch or knit too many stitches together. Don't panic, just fake it. At the end of the row, if you have two stitches and you're only supposed to have one, just knit them together. No one will ever notice.

SHAWL

Beginning with deeper ruffle at bottom of shawl, cast on 1,200 stitches (you can do it).

Row 1: Knit each stitch to end of row.

Row 2: Purl each stitch to end of row.

Row 3: Knit each stitch to end of row.

Row 4: Purl 1, * yarn over, purl 2 together *, repeat from * to * to last stitch, purl 1.

Row 5: Knit each stitch to end of row.

Row 6: Purl each stitch to end of row.

Row 7: * Knit 2 together *, repeat from * to * to end of row—600 stitches (it's getting easier already).

Row 8: Purl 1, * yarn over, purl 2 together *, repeat from * to * to last stitch, purl 1.

Row 9: Knit each stitch to end of row.

Row 10: Purl each stitch to end of row.

Row 11: * Knit 2 together *, repeat from * to * to end of row—300 stitches (piece of cake).

Body of shawl in an all-over lace pattern:

Row 1: Purl 1, * yarn over, purl 2 together *, repeat from * to * to last stitch, purl 1.

Row 2: Knit each stitch to end of row.

Row 3: Purl each stitch to end of row.

Row 4: Knit each stitch to end of row.

Rows 1 to 4 make up the lace pattern for the body of the shawl. Repeat these four rows 20 more times (a total of 84 rows).

Narrower ruffle at top of shawl:

Row 1: Purl 1, * yarn over, purl 2 together *, repeat from * to * to last stitch, purl 1.

Row 2: Knit into the front and back of every stitch, including the yarnovers—600 stitches (getting a little hot in here).

Row 3: Knit into the front and back of every stitch—1,200 stitches (déjà vu all over again).

Row 4: Knit each stitch to end of row.

Row 5: Bind off in knit stitch (even though you will be on a purl side).

FINISHING

Using the blunt-end yarn needle, weave in all ends. Don't block this shawl. Also, be sure to store it flat, not hanging, so it doesn't stretch out of shape.

IN BOUCLÉ

You can use this versatile pattern to experiment with a wide variety of yarns—just use a needle that is the same size or slightly larger than the recommendation on the label. To make the shawl shorter (end to end), cast on fewer stitches. Just be sure that you always work with an even number of stitches. The basic pattern is the same. This version is knit with a lustrous silk bouclé yarn that's approximately the same weight but has a rougher texture. Use the same size needle but cast on fewer stitches, since this yarn knits at a slightly heavier gauge. To make the same size shawl, you'll need about 750 yards (683 m). If you want to make a shorter shawl that is about 50" (127 cm) long, cast on 800 stitches.

YARN

Lightweight boucle yarn
106 yd (97 m)

NEEDLES

• Size 6 (4 mm) circular needle or size needed to obtain gauge, at least 40" (102) long

GAUGE

• 16 stitches = 4" (10 cm) in lace stitch

KNITTING CLASS

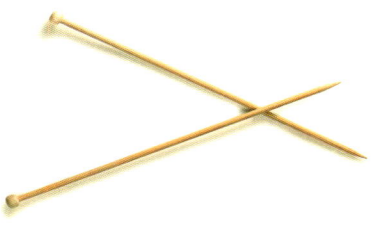

CASTING ON BIG TIME

You need to cast on 1,200 stitches, so how long should the tail be? Try this:

Wrap the yarn around the needle 12 times. Take the yarn off and measure it. It should be about 8" (20.5 cm) long and that's $1/100$ the length you will need in total (1,200 stitches divided by 12). So, 8" (20.5 cm) × 100 = 800" (2,050 cm) or 66 feet (201 m). Using the Five Foot Rule, that would mean stretching the yarn from fingertip to fingertip about 13 to 14 times. Throw in a couple extra fingertip stretches. It would be far better to waste a few feet of yarn than to have to start casting on all over again.

TIP Do you know the Five Foot Rule? With arms outstretched, fingertip to fingertip on the average woman is about five feet. I usually allow 1 to 1¼ (2.5 to 3.2 cm) of yarn per stitch for the tail when I'm casting on with medium-weight yarn. If my scarf has 120 stitches, that's 120 inches (305 cm) or 10 feet (3 m). Using the Five Foot Rule, that's two fintertip-to-fingertip stretches with a little extra thrown in for insurance.

1

How in the world do you keep count of 1,200 stitches to cast on? Just get it right 100 stitches at a time.

1. Cut a contrast yarn into 11 pieces, each 4" (10 cm) long, to make stitch markers. Tie each piece into a loop, using an overhand knot.

2. Cast on 100 stitches and double-check to make sure you're correct. Now, put a marker in between these stitches and the next 100 (just slip the stitch marker over the needle). You know all the stitches to the right of the marker are correctly counted. Remember to remove the stitch markers when you knit the first row.

2

Cables and Lace Scarf

Hand-painted luxury yarn works beautifully with this easy cable. The lace panels keep the knitting lightweight and the scarf drapes beautifully. Also, the design looks attractive on both sides.

FINISHED MEASUREMENTS

7½" wide x 56" long (19.1 x 142 cm)

GAUGE

- 17 stitches and 24 rows = 4" (10 cm) in stockinette stitch
- 22 stitches and 22 rows = 4" (10 cm) in cable pattern

MATERIALS

- Medium weight multifiber yarn, approx 370 yd (338 m)

NEEDLES AND NOTIONS

- Size 8 (5 mm) needles or size necessary to obtain gauge
- Cable needle
- Yarn needle for weaving in ends

BEGINNING SECTION

Cast on 37 stitches.

Row 1 (RS): K1, yo, p2tog, k3, *[p2tog, yo] twice, k3 *; repeat from * to * until last 3 stitches, p2tog, yo, k1.

Row 2: K3, *p1, inc, p1, k4*; repeat from * to * until last 6 stitches, p1, inc, p1, k3—42 sts. (Note that increases are worked in purl stitches.)

MAIN SECTION

Follow the Scarf Chart below.

Row 3: K1, yo, p2tog, 4-ST RKC, *[yo, p2tog] (twice), 4-ST RKC *; repeat from * to * until last 3 stitches, p2tog, yo, k1.

Row 4: K3, *p4, k4*; repeat from * to * until last 7 stitches, p4, k3.

Row 5: K1, yo, p2tog, k4, *[p2tog, yo] (twice), k4*; repeat from * to * until last 3 stitches, p2tog, yo, k1.

Row 6: K3, *p4, k4*; repeat from * to * until last 7 stitches, p4, k3.

Repeat rows 3 – 6 until scarf measures about 55$\frac{1}{2}$" (141 cm) or desired length, ending with a row 3.

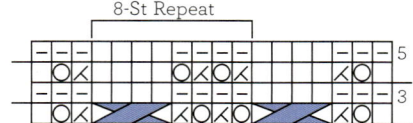

ENDING SECTION

Decrease Row (WS): K3, *p1, p2tog, p1, k4*; repeat from * to * until last 7 stitches, p1, p2tog, p1, k3—37 sts.

Next Row: K1, yo, p2tog, k3 *[p2tog, yo] twice, k3 *; repeat from * to * until last 3 stitches, p2tog, yo, k1.

Bind off all stitches in pattern.

FINISHING

Using the yarn needle, weave in all ends. If desired, very lightly steam block using a steam iron on a wool setting. Don't let the iron come any closer than 3" (7.6 cm) to your knitting. Steam just enough to relax the selvedge edges.

In order to make the cast-on and bound-off edges of the scarf lay flat, a few different rows are worked at the beginning and end. This will increase the stitches at the beginning and decrease the stitches at the end.

Hot Sauce

RIBBON KNITTED IN LACE STITCH

This sassy red shawl is the perfect complement to your little black dress. Knitted with a beautiful ribbon yarn, it has just a touch of metallic. The directions combine two knitting skills: knitting a triangle shape by increasing on every other row, and knitting in a simple lace pattern. This pattern can be just a bit complicated to learn, and it's intimidating to start right in on expensive ribbon. Use some plain yarn from your stash to learn and practice the pattern first. If you want a larger shawl, continue the pattern until you've reached the size you want.

YARN

- Bulky-weight ribbon yarn: 165 yd (166 m)

NEEDLES AND NOTIONS

- Size 15 (10 mm) circular needle or size needed to obtain gauge, at least 24" (61 cm) long
- Size 17 (12.75 mm) circular or singlepoint needles or size needed to obtain gauge
- Blunt-end yarn needle
- 3 large-hole gold beads
- Large-eye beading needle for pulling yarn through beads

GAUGE

- 8 stitches and 16 rows = 4" (10 cm) in lace stitch

FINISHED SIZE

- 17" × 39" (43 × 99 cm), not including tassels

TIP Knitting with ribbon is only difficult if you make it so. The ribbon doesn't need to lie flat for every stitch or align any particular way. As you knit, the ribbon might twist or fold over for a while. That's okay; it will just enhance the texture of your knitted fabric. Remember, knitting should be relaxing, not stressful.

SHAWL

Using the smaller needle, cast on 4 stitches.

Row 1: Knit each stitch to end of row.

Row 2: Knit 1, yarn over, purl 2, yarn over, knit 1—6 stitches.

Row 3: Knit 1, * yarn over, purl 2 together *, repeat from * to * until last stitch, knit 1.

Row 4: Knit 1, yarn over, purl 1, * yarn over, purl 2 together *, repeat from * to * until 2 stitches remain, purl 1, yarn over, knit 1.

Repeat rows 3 and 4 until the desired width, leaving about 6 yd (5.5 m) for binding off. Bind off very loosely using the larger needle.

You increase your stitch count only on the even numbered rows. It's really helpful to know which side you are on in case you put your knitting down and can't remember. As you begin making your shawl, use a safety pin to mark the side of your knitting with even numbered rows. Then if you can't remember what side you are on, just look for the pin.

FINISHING

Using the blunt-end yarn needle, weave in all ends. You don't need to block this scarf. If it seems a little stiff, mist it lightly with water and allow the scarf to dry on a flat, towel-covered surface.

TASSELS

1. Cut two pieces of yarn, each 36" (91.5 cm) long. These will be the long tassels at the side points of the shawl.

2. Working one side at a time, thread one piece of yarn through the shawl point. Even up the ends and use the beading needle to pull the ends through the bead one at a time.

3. To make the tassel at the back, cut two pieces of yarn, each 12" (30.5 cm) long. Thread both pieces through the back point. Even up the yarn ends and then thread through the eye of the bead one at a time (you may need to use the large-eye beading needle).

4. Trim the ends of all the yarns to even up and remove frayed edges as necessary.

Crazy Lace Knitting

The foundation of all lace knitting is the eyelet stitch, a yarn-over increase paired with a decrease, usually by knitting two stitches together [yo, k2tog], which makes deliberate holes in the final fabric. You can use a multitude of variations of how and when the yarn-over and decrease pair is done to create different lace effects. Decreases are commonly done in a specific direction, slanting to the left or to the right to create directional lines in the fabric along with the holes, which can be used for specific effects. Making this crazy lace sampler scarf is a perfect way to discover and understand how lace knitting works since the patterns are fairly easy and change frequently.

Lace patterns are created by repeating the same stitch instructions across a row in a specific multiple that equals the final stitch count for the row. Some patterns are very simple and are repeated over a few stitches, while others repeat over many stitches and a number of rows.

An easy way to read lace patterns is by using lace charts that often accompany the written instructions. Charts are read in the same direction as you knit; each horizontal line of squares indicates the total stitch count for that row of knitting, and the number of vertical rows indicate each row of knitting required for the pattern repeat. Charts start at the lower right corner and are read from right to left on right side (odd rows), and from left to right on wrong side (even rows). Many charts, like the ones included for this pattern, only indicate odd rows since each wrong side row is purled across.

Each square on a chart contains a symbol, which is an instruction. The symbols themselves are usually a visual representation of the stitch to be done; a yarn-over is an open O, a k2tog is a line that slants to the right. Lace charts include a legend that indicates what instruction each symbol represents. Once you get used to reading charts, you'll easily recognize the symbols. For decreases, the direction of the symbol's slant is the direction of the slant of the decrease. Any method you want to use to achieve the desired direction is perfectly fine as long as it's facing the same way.

Feel free to mix the patterns as you wish, repeating each chart as desired over as many inches of the sampler as you'd like. Throw in a row or two of basic eyelet (k2tog, yo) or a garter ridge to delineate each section if you wish. Most importantly, have fun with it!

Crazy Lace Sampler Scarf

BY MYRA WOOD

PATTERN NOTE:

For a finished, chain stitch selvage:
(all rows except first set-up row)
Knit the first stitch through the back loop and slip the last stitch purlwise, with the yarn in the front. This is done on every row, regardless of whether it is the right or wrong side and is not included in the pattern instructions.

WHAT YOU'LL NEED . . . .

YARN

- Fingering or sock yarn, any matching weight and content

NEEDLES

- Size 7 needles, straight or circular

NOTIONS

- stitch markers
- yarn needle

INSTRUCTIONS

Cast on 32 sts.

Set-up Row 1: K4, pm, k24, pm, k4.

Set-up Row 2: Knit.

Row 1 and every odd row: K1, k2tog, yo, k1, sm, work center 24 stitches, sm, k1, yo, ssk, k1.

Row 2 and every even row: K4, sm, work evenly (k, and/or p) to next marker, sm, k4

Continue as follows:

On each odd row, use one of the charts below, repeating across the row the required times for the center stitches. Repeat that stitch pattern as many times as desired until you want to switch patterns. Pick any other chart and start the new pattern or combine rows of plain garter as breaks between patterns. Include rows of plain eyelet [k2tog, yo] and double yarn overs, dropping the second wrap on the next even row. Textured stitches such as cables and bobbles can also be included. Check stitch guides for lace patterns with multiples of 4, 6, 12 or 24 to use as well. Consider knitting one half of the scarf as the sampler and the other half in just one stitch pattern. Change yarns as you change patterns if you like. A few rows of novelty yarn in garter stitch looks great. Mix it up and go crazy!

Charts and instructions for Right Side Rows ONLY

R1 (RS): K1, yo, sl1 k2tog psso, yo
R3: Yo, sl1 k2tog psso, yo, k1

R1 (RS): K2, k2tog, yo
R3: K1, k2tog, yo, k1
R5: K2tog, yo, k2
R7: K1, ssk, yo, k1
R9: K2, ssk, yo

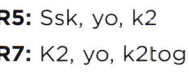

R1 (RS): Ssk, yo, k2
R3: K2, yo, k2tog
R5: Ssk, yo, k2
R7: K2, yo, k2tog

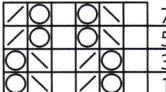

R1 (RS): K1, yo, k2tog, k1, ssk, yo
R3: K1, yo, k2tog, k1, ssk, yo
R5: K1, ssk, yo, k1, yo, k2tog
R7: K1, ssk, yo, k1, yo, k2tog

R1 (RS): K6
R3: K1, ssk, yo, k1, yo, k2tog
R5: K1, yo, sl1 k2tog psso, yo, k2tog, yo
R7: K2, yo, sl1 k2tog psso, yo, k1

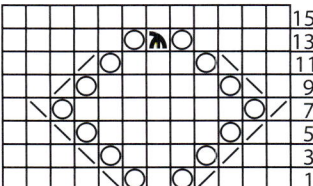

R1 (RS): K3, k2tog, yo, k1, yo, ssk, k4
R3: K2, k2tog, yo, k3, yo, ssk, k3
R5: K1, k2tog, yo, k5, yo, ssk, k2
R7: K2tog, yo, k7, yo, ssk, k1
R9: K1, ssk, yo, k5, yo, k2tog, k2
R11: K2, ssk, yo, k3, yo, k2tog, k3
R13: K4, yo, sl1 k2tog psso, yo, k5
R15: K12

R1 (RS): Yo, ssk, k1, k2tog, yo, k1
R3: K1, yo, sl1 k2tog psso, yo, k2
R5: K2, yo, k3
R7: K6

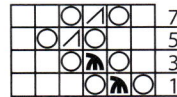

R1 (RS): Yo, sl1 k2tog psso, yo, k3
R3: K1, yo, sl1 k2tog psso, yo, k2
R5: K2, yo, k3tog, yo, k1
R7: K1, yo, k3tog, yo, k2

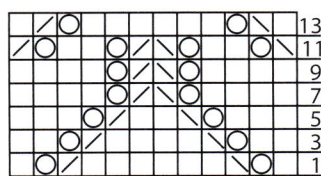

R1 (RS): K1, yo, ssk, k6, k2tog, yo, k1
R3: K2, yo, ssk, k4, k2tog, yo, k2
R5: K3, yo, ssk, k2, k2tog, yo, k3
R7: K4, yo, ssk, k2tog, yo, k4
R9: K4, yo, ssk, k2tog, yo, k4
R11: Ssk, yo, k2, yo, ssk, k2tog, yo, k2, yo, k2tog
R13: K1, ssk, yo, k6, yo, k2tog, k1

Lace Curtain Panels

These scalloped-edged curtain panels are created using a traditional lace pattern known as fishtail lace. The basic pattern can easily be modified to fit any window in your home. The panels are finished with a rod casing at the top.

WHAT YOU'LL LEARN . . . .

- How to make a multiple-row lace pattern with traveling yarnover (yo) holes
- How to make a casing with a turning row and hem

WHAT YOU'LL NEED . . . .

YARN

- Medium weight, smooth yarn, approx. 400 yd (366 m). If possible, find a yarn that has some bamboo or rayon as a portion of the fiber content. This will give the curtain panels better drape.

NEEDLES AND NOTIONS

- US size 7 (4.5 mm) circular needle at least 29" (74 cm) long, or size needed to achieve gauge
- US size 8 (5 mm) straight or circular needle one size larger than smaller needle used to obtain gauge
- Yarn needle for weaving in ends and stitching casing
- Rust-proof T-pins for blocking

EQUIPMENT

- Iron
- Ironing board
- Curtain rod

GAUGE

- 20 sts = 4" (10 cm) in stockinette stitch

How to Knit the Lace Curtain Panels (make two)

FINISHED DIMENSIONS (FOR EACH SIDE)

- 15" (38 cm) wide by 16" (41 cm) long

It's easy to modify the size of the curtain panels. Each repeat of the lace pattern is 10 stitches and about 2" (5 cm) wide. If you want to make the panel wider, then add stitches in multiples of 10. You can also adjust the length by completing fewer or more repeats of the basic 8-row pattern.

TIP Slip the stitch markers as you come to them. Until you become comfortable with the pattern, it helps to count the 10 stitches in each section after completion.

1 Using the larger needle, **cast on** 75 stitches. Switch to the smaller needle and work a set-up row, placing markers (pm) to delineate the lace pattern repeats, as follows: K2, [pm, k10] 7 times, pm, k3.

2 Begin the fishtail lace pattern. Each repeat is 10 stitches wide from side to side, and 8 rows are required to complete one pattern repeat from bottom to top. When working even-numbered, wrong side (WS) rows, slip markers as you come to them.

Row 1 (RS): K3, *sm, yo, k3, s1, k2tog, psso, k3, yo, k1*; repeat from * to * until 2 sts remain, sm, k2.

Row 2: K3, p until 3 sts remain, k3.

Row 3: K3, *k1, yo, k2, s1, k2tog, psso, k2, yo, k2*; repeat from * to * until 2 sts remain, k2.

Row 4: K3, p until 3 sts remain, k3.

Row 5: K3,*k2, yo, k1, s1, k2tog, psso, k1, yo, k3*; repeat from * to * until 2 sts remain, k2.

Row 6: K3, p until 3 sts remain, k3.

Row 7: K3, *k3, yo, s1, k2tog, psso, yo, k4*; repeat from * to * until 2 sts remain, k2.

Row 8: K3, p until 3 sts remain, k3.

3 You have completed the first full repeat (8 rows) of the lace pattern. Repeat rows 1 through 8 nine more times for a total of ten repeats. Now a short section of stockinette stitch is made to form the front of the casing. All of the markers can be removed at this point. You may find it easier to mark off the first 3 and last 3 stitches with a marker so you can remember to knit them on the wrong-side (purl) rows.

Row 1 (RS): Knit.

Row 2: K3, p until 3 sts remain, k3.

Repeat rows 1 and 2 four more times.

4 A purl row is made on the right side of the knitting. The purl bumps create a turning row, a natural fold line for the knitting.

Next row: Purl.

5 Switch to the larger needles and work a few more rows of stockinette stitch.

Row 1: K3, p until 3 sts remain, k3.

Row 2: Knit.

Repeat rows 1 and 2 three more times.

Next row: Knit

Bind off all stitches loosely and evenly. Weave in all loose ends.

Curtain Rod Casing

6 To make the casing, fold the top edge along the purl turning row and pin in place.

7 Sew casing into place using a whip stitch: Thread about 1 yd (0.9 m) of yarn on a yarn needle; don't knot the yarn, but leave a tail about 8" (20 cm) that will be woven in later. Starting on the right edge, insert the needle into one bump of a stitch on the wrong side and then into one loop cn the cast-off edge. Continue across the edge from right to left working whip stitches between the purl bumps and the cast-off loops. Work a few extra stitches on each edge and then weave in the ends.

Block following the directions on page 7 for blocking lace.

6

7